199 Ideas and Suggestions to
Honor and Love Your Wife

Bob Vickers, Rod Casey
and Jeff Sharland

*Here are over 199 practical, simple, mostly common-sense, easy-to-read-and-understand ideas and suggestions to start the work...
or to make a change!*

Caution: Following these suggestions
will change your life...and your wife's!

WinePress Publishing
MUKILTEO, WA 98275

199 Ideas and Suggestions to Honor and Love Your Wife
Copyright © 1997 by Robert Vickers and Jeff Sharland

Published by WinePress Publishing
PO Box 1406
Mukilteo, WA 98275

Cover by **DENHAM**DESIGN, Everett, WA

Unless otherwise noted, Scripture quotations are from the *Holy Bible: New International Version*. Copyright © 1973, 1978, 1984 by the International Bible Society.

Printed in the United States of America.

Library of Congress Catalog Card Number: 97-60626
ISBN 1-57921-021-X

Comments from Readers on Previous Editions

—∽∽—

"I must say that I think *199 Ideas and Suggestions to Honor and Love Your Wife* is full of simple, common-sense stuff and I don't think it should be necessary to print. However, it is making a tremendous difference in the relationships and lives of several men in my church as they seek to change the way they relate to their individual wives. Please send me three more copies to give to upcoming grooms I am scheduled to marry this Fall. Do you have anything similar for women? Thanks!"

—Pastor in Ohio

"Thank you for providing simple and practical ideas for me to love my wife. Providing suggestions in different topic areas helped me to be better prepared to love her in ways that were meaningful in a variety of ways."

—Police Officer in Washington, D.C.

"My father takes three new ideas each week and applies them to his relationship with my mother (they've been married 45 years). It's the first time I've heard or seen him express love for her. It is truly changing his heart and I weep when I see it. He even applies the concepts to me, my five siblings and his seven grandchildren. How can I adequately say thank you for the wonderful little book?!"

—Proud daughter in Iowa

"A great tool to help you love your wife—practically—in ways that communicate to her."

—Roger Fleming, National Director of Business and Professional Ministries, The Navigators, Colorado Springs, Colorado

"Thank you for your great little book! I use it in group settings and find it to be great discussion material. I have seen it used by God to save marriages and make a difference in many others! Thank You!"
—Jim Riley, Marital Counselor/Family Therapist, Original Member No-Name Defense & Miami Dolphins/World Champions of 1972, Edmond, Oklahoma

"We must break the cycle of marital relationships that we see perpetuated in our society! *199 Ideas and Suggestions to Honor and Love Your Wife* is a wonderful place to start. But men must be told that it takes "balance." They must love and honor their wife in many different ways and unconditionally! You've done a great job!"
—Author from Arizona

"My daughter was three weeks old when I was given a copy of your book and my wife and I were separated already. She kept asking me for help, so I kept sending her cards and flowers... I didn't know what else to do. I didn't have a clue how to love and honor my wife or help her. Well, after three weeks of reading and rereading your book and practicing the suggestions, my wife accepted me back into the marriage and we are happier than ever. You know, it feels great to love and honor her!"
—New Father in Ohio

"I have seen these type of 'list books' quite a bit—I even own 7 or 8 of them myself. But yours is different because it gives men lists of ideas and suggestions, but then explains why to do it, how to do it and what a difference it will make. It even gives some elementary help for those too stubborn to think on their own! Thanks for your contribution!"
—Minister and Family Counselor in Kansas City, Missouri

"Your book is a great little piece of work. It is full of common-sense stuff that I used to do very regularly. However, after 12 years of marriage, I'm ashamed to say I haven't kept it up. I have two copies—one in my briefcase and one on my desk. I regularly pick it up, thumb through it and try new ideas. After 6 weeks, my wife is responding like never before. It has really 'lit' our relationship! Thanks!"

—From Colorado

"Daddy, thank you for writing a book about big-people stuff for me and Ben and Audrey and David and Daniel and Laura and Andrew. Can you write one for kids?"

—Proud daughter of one of the authors (Yes, angel, one is available on how to honor and love your children!)

Bob's Dedication

To the most important people in my life.

My wife, Laura: Thank you for loving me. Thank you for taking the time to show me how to love you back. Thank you for the many times that you have practiced "modeling" the love that you have given to me, our children, friends and clients and strangers. Thank you for forgiving me when I have failed and for communicating to me how I can be a better husband, father, man and friend. Thank you for sharing your life and love with me. I love you, honey and I'm committed to you.

My daughters, Audrey and Allison: Audrey, you are at an age where decisions for your lifetime have been influenced and mostly established. I pray that I have been a positive example for you. Allis, angel, hold out for relationships in which you are loved and honored. Sweetheart, you are a precious gift from God and I treasure the opportunity and responsibility of being your father and "daddy." I love you both with all my heart more than you'll ever know.

My sons, Andrew, Benjamin, David and Daniel: Andrew, I miss you, I love you and I am who I am today because of you. Thank you for your love and your life. Benjamin, I pray that you will see me love and honor people enough that it comes very natural for you in life. Please don't ever hesitate to ask someone for help in learning and knowing how to love. I love you a lot, son and I am proud to be your dad, to tickle you, protect you, love you and teach you to "do life." David and Daniel, I have tried to model the love and honor for your mother that is contained in this booklet. I pray that you will also exhibit this behavior to significant people in your life.

My friends: My friends and "family" in my Accountability, Care and Growth Groups; Columbia's WoodCrest Chapel; and all my "fellow travelers and strugglers." Especially to Jeff Sharland and Dale Swoboda, "Thanks for dreaming together. To God be the Glory!" To Marshall Robb, "Thanks for reaching out and asking." To Russ, Fitz, Rod and Pieter, "Thanks for teaching, leading and modeling." And to my natural, earthly family, especially Uncle Max, "Thanks for modeling a lifetime of Godliness and obedience that I am only now comprehending." This Okie loves ya'll alot!

Rod's Dedication

To Julie
who has given
more love and understanding
than this man deserves
or could have ever
dreamed of...

I love you!

Jeff's Dedication

To Dana,
my partner
for these many years.

Thank you
for sharing life
with me
and making me
what I am.

I love you!

TABLE OF CONTENTS

ACKNOWLEDGMENTS

Special thanks to:

The Institute for Encouragement, including: Dr. Dale Swoboda, Nancy-Rebecca Palmer, Larry Gates, Pieter Van Waarde, Dr. Mark Fuhrman, Teresa Parker and all who planted seeds through their work. Thank you from our hearts. May God increase your reward in Heaven!

Bill Vickers at Otis Phillips Printing, Enid, Oklahoma, Rod Dent and David Mueller, Jim and Robin Riley, Bishop Phil Porter, The Promise Keepers Organization, Athena Dean and WinePress Publishing, and to the authors of books and tapes on relationships (Appendix H).

Reviewers of drafts who provided invaluable feedback:

Laura Vickers
Dale and Georgalu Swoboda
Dana Sharland
Marshall Robb
Larry Gates
David Mueller
Teresa Parker
LaVonne and Mike Way
Larry Markway
Larry Glabe
Pieter Van Waarde
Terry Hatridge
Dr. Mark Fuhrman

INTRODUCTION

This is a working draft of a document that will never be finished because the work will never be completed. When we got married, we publicly chose to love and honor our wives and engaged in a 99-year plan to accomplish *it*.

What is *it*?

It is our individual promise, made in front of "God and all these witnesses," to love, honor and cherish the woman that we said "I do" to.

But few men have taught or adequately demonstrated how to do *it*. After all, we provided for our family, protected them and frequently told them that we love them. Yet, loving and honoring our wife and children were far from what we were doing.

This is a working attempt to relate some of the ideas of how to love and honor our respective wives that we have found to work in our situations. We want to share our efforts at doing *it* in hopes of helping others make progress in their journey, as well.

This book became reality because we simply wanted to help men learn new ideas on how to honor and love their wives.

This is not a checklist-type book. We don't advocate that you try to do everything. It is designed to help you think about the way you show love and honor to your wife. If you already are successful in this area, congratulations! Research shows, however, that you are among a minority of men who know how to and do, honor and love their wives. You can think of this book as a way to provide some additional ideas that you might consider to make something great...even greater.

However, for the rest of you who truly desire to love and honor your wife, this book provides some simple, basic, mostly common-sense ideas and suggestions to begin the process of changing your heart. The goal is to *change the heart*.

It is not good enough to do things of honor for/to your wife and that is not what we are saying at all. It's about *being* honorable for/to your wife.

The transformation, in our opinion, is in the acts of love and honor that we choose to do because she is our wife, regardless of feelings or emotions. We choose fact over feeling because we made that commitment on the day we were married—and suspect you did, too.

It's also about balance. We must learn to love and honor our wife through all of the interactions we have with her or with others concerning her!

There are several unique features about this book.

1) Brevity. It is written for you to spend a few minutes at a time to work on behavior and the transformation of your heart.

2) It provides an explanation after each of the ideas or suggestions. Some, however, cannot be explained…just do them. We know that is a bit trite, but men and women don't think alike and for a man to understand and think like a woman simply isn't possible.

3) It provides "helps" in the Appendix. Research again tells us that most men truly desire to honor and love their wives, but they haven't the slightest idea what that means or where to begin. Well, we have tried to help you know what it means and where to begin.

4) It is small enough to carry in your briefcase, Bible, back pocket or wherever! It's OK to conceal it and read it when no one knows. Keep it handy at all times and become proactive in honoring and loving your wife. It will take you a long time to convince your wife that your change is from your heart and is real, but seek Godly wisdom, seek to be consistent and seek God's help in loving your wife as Christ loves the church.

Think of the impact that you will have on others as you seek to honor and love this woman; the testimony to your children of love for their mother, other people that you work with, others that your wife works with, neighbors, others from your church and on and on and on. Consequently, it is important for you to start and really mean business!

This book is not intended to be a final authority. Nor is it intended *in any way* to put down women and their equality in our society, in our relationships and under God. Rather, it is a good-faith effort to help other men love and honor their wives.

So, please read the following ideas and suggestions. Don't try to do all of them at once. Just try to find a few at a time that are new and different and *start* the work. We pray that you and your wife receive something meaningful from your work. And, as you see the fruit, expand your horizon. Try other ideas and suggestions and share with others.

Then, write us and let us know. Let us know if they work for you or what comments would better empower you to do the work. Also, let us know additional ideas that work for you and we'll pass them on to help others.

So, men, take the challenge of Stephen Covey in *Seven Habits of Highly Effective People*:

"My friend, love is a verb. Love the feeling—is a fruit of love, the verb. So love her... Serve her... Sacrifice... Listen to her... Empathize... Appreciate... Affirm her... Are you willing to do that?"

In Ephesians 5:25, we are told, "Husbands, love your wives just as Christ loved the church." Following are 199-plus ways to begin the work. Go for it!

We have tried to categorize the ideas in a simple way. We begin with ideas and suggestions for you to work on within yourself. This first area is critical! Please read through the ideas and suggestions carefully and ponder your own situation. Work on them primarily between yourself and God. However, remember, take care of yourself so that you can take care of others. Working on yourself is a lifelong process beginning now and lasting forever. These first ideas are intended to help you do that.

We then turn to ideas and suggestions on how to honor and love your wife through several categories, including:

- Create and continually enhance meaning and value for her.
- Encourage her with your words.
- Give her your undivided attention.
- Serve her and share responsibilities.
- Physically adore, honor and love her.

- Shower her with gifts.
- Just because you love her.

The goal of all of this is for you to *change your heart* toward your wife. Doing these things will not automatically mean you are a great, Godly husband. Rather, taking action and actively loving and honoring your wife is a way to be obedient in your commitment to Christ.

BEGIN BY WORKING ON YOURSELF

—∽∽—

Gary Smalley, Tim Sledge and Dr. Russ Hardesty, among many others, have dedicated their professional lives to helping people "Take care of yourself *so that* you can then take care of others." They empower people with the ability to move beyond the pain of their past, confront and embrace themselves and their situations, restore relationships of all types and empower individuals to have fruitful futures. They assist people to encounter God and experience unconditional grace, mercy and love (as well as eternal life).

We believe that you must take care of your own issues in order to be able to engage in the process of loving and honoring your wife or anyone/anything else. Most often, this is a process that is never complete. However, any dysfunction can be addressed and you can learn to deal with your issues.

Therefore, we believe a first step is to work on yourself. Consequently, before looking at the ideas and suggestions on honoring and loving your wife, please spend some time in this section on working on yourself.

This, by no means, is a complete list. We simply want to provide a few ideas for you to begin the process and not all will apply for every person! Be realistic and seek to improve yourself. Remember to use a vertical standard and not a horizontal one!

If you want changes, you must make them happen. Most often, however, we can achieve the changes and make them last by beginning within our own hearts, minds and lives.

A.
Ask God for Help.

Ask God to help you deal with your life experiences and straighten them out if need be. Maybe you will need to first meet Him in a personal experience. Maybe you need for Him to help you in a good, old-fashioned cleansing and repentance. Confess sin, repent and seek to walk in newness of His Life.

B.
Continuously Work on Yourself!

This is probably the greatest gift you can give your wife. Do it for her, do it for the kids, do it for yourself or just do it. Get involved in a male accountability group. This shows her that you love her and honor her enough that you want to make some changes in your own life, too. She will probably take the initiative to do the same thing for herself. Appendix G is a list of do's and don'ts. Read them over and think about them. Then, work on them.

Appendix J is a list of books—Christian and secular—that would serve as a good starting point for you. Many of them are available as a "book on tape." So if reading is difficult for you, get one on tape.

Appendix H is a list of other resources for you to consider or contact for further information. Most offer books, newsletters or magazines. Many offer marital workshops. Some offer counseling and/or referral services.

C.
Be Responsible for Your Mistakes!

Don't always make your wife feel like she has made all the mistakes. Accept personal responsibility for your decisions, errors or choices and acknowledge them. Work at learning the following words and practice saying them. Make it a goal to say them *every day*!

"I'm sorry." "I was wrong!" "I made a mistake." "Will you forgive me?" "I love you, sweetheart!" (or honey, love-muffin, etc.)

When you say these things, you must mean them! Then, seek to change. Don't repeat a wrong or continue making the same mistakes.

D.
Keep Your Word.

If you said you would do something, do it. Write it in your schedule immediately and make it a priority above all others because it is a commitment to your wife and/or family.

E.
Quit Whining!
About money, health, job, being tired, kids' behavior, etc.

F.
Model Desired Behavior...
...Rather than demand it. Start with honor, love, obedience, patience and submission. Then try honesty, openness, gentleness, service, cleaning, etc. Model these character traits and qualities. You'll be surprised how your wife and children will pick up on them, begin to practice them and incorporate them into their own lives.

G.
Pray for Wisdom.
Pray for God to give you wisdom, patience and creative abilities to know how to give your wife significant affirmation and encouragement in a way that *she* understands, needs and desires. He can give you the thoughts, words and abilities to accomplish this, but you must ask Him. Ask Him to make it very clear to you. Ask Him to show you ways that you can understand. But don't sit around and wait. Just begin to love and honor her NOW!

H.
Check Your Heart's Motive.
Always ask yourself, "What is my motive, and how can it help give value to my wife?" Discuss your self-evaluation with your wife. *Confess your faults* and ask for her help. Assure her, however, that you are pursuing help from an *accountability* person or group in addition to her input. We don't want to de-emphasize the importance of this one at all. It is important for you to seek to have integrity and pure motives with everyone, not just your wife. However, we are trying to assure you of the importance it has in the marital relationship. A *pure motive* will be consistent whether she is around or not, she is aware of your behaviors or not, or she is directly benefitting or not. Think about this!

I.
Pray for Discernment.
Pray that God will help you learn how to love her and discern what is important and what is not. Ask Him to help you discern what would

be meaningful to your wife. It will take time...but you can learn how. Ask God to restore you to the pure and undefiled love that you once experienced with her (or ask Him to give it like *never* before).

J.
Develop Integrity.

Integrity infers many traits, including: predictability, reliability, dependability, trust, accountability...

Can she predict your responses to a variety of circumstances? Are you consistent and reliable? Can she come to you and depend on you to help her or meet her needs? Are you trustworthy? Do you keep your word? Does your *walk* match your *talk* at all times? Work on these things, and periodically ask her for an evaluation.

K.
Distinguish Between What is Important and What is Urgent...

...And then learn to act proactively. Often we spend an incredible amount of time doing what is urgent and rarely accomplish those things that are important. *Be proactive!*

L.
Accept Her Love as Given.

1) Love her the way she needs for you to.
2) Accept her love as given.

Both of these are self-denial approaches for you, but they are the most rewarding steps you will ever take in your relationship with your wife. She is not perfect! And, Thank God, she isn't like you! You were brought together and united to *complete* each other, not to *compete* with each other.

M.
Don't Take Office Frustrations Home.

Even after a long, hard, frustrating day, go home and put on a *Hollywood act*. It isn't her fault your day was bad!

N.
Improve the Gift of Yourself that You Give Her.

Read Kent Hughes' *Disciplines of a Godly Man* (Appendix J) or another similar book at least twice a year. *You* take the initiative to ask your pastor, a friend, a bookstore clerk or someone to recommend a good book. Seek to develop a quality quiet time, prayer life and Godly journey.

O.
Be a Responsible Father.

Get up and check on the kids when they cry in the middle of the night, when it is extremely cold to be sure they are covered, when it is stormy to check if they are awake, etc. (Appendix H and Appendix J for parenting books and resources). Children are a gift from God. Be responsible and interested in working with her to receive and respect these precious gifts from Him. And remember, a child's life, however brief, is a celebration!

P.
Learn to Not Be a Perfectionist.

Expectations can kill a relationship. This is true for friendships, marriages and parenting relationships! Be specific about your needs and be patient when they are unmet. Avoid *perfectionism*!

Q.
Be Careful with Humor.

A sense of humor is a treasured gift from God. However, learn when the application of a sense of humor is appropriate and when it isn't. It can be a tremendous release and a blessing, but it can also be an incredible hindrance and even a curse. Learn the difference. However, never joke about her faults, her weight or her family!

R.
Ask for Directions.

When you're in the car together—and lost—*you* suggest that you should stop and ask for directions. Then, stop and ask for help. Part of this solution may be to pray for a *teachable spirit* or a *learning spirit*. Don't let pride and arrogance rob you of this sort of exchange with your wife.

S.
Continually Grow Yourself.

Maintain male accountability and growth groups and strong, spiritual male friends that can help you work on areas of *your* life and hold you accountable. Continually grow.

T.
Pray for Understanding.

Pray that God will show you her needs and how to meet them. You will never *totally understand* her. The two of you simply are different and think differently! But pray to get a better understanding of her and how you can love and honor her in a meaningful way.

U.
Do Your Own Chores!

Assume responsibility for your share of household chores regardless of how much you work outside of the home! Vacuum, dust, clean the windows, change the sheets, etc. Do your share *plus some.*

V.
Learn to Say "No" When Asked to Be Involved in Everything.

Community service, church work or employer-related activities are not bad. However, learn to say "no" to some things in order to spend time with your wife and/or family. Use your family as an excuse and make sure that you express that it is "my decision to keep family time important." Then, *spend the time with your family.* OK, this will be hard for some of you, but this applies to golf games, softball, football and other sporting and social events. Learn to honor and respect your wife and family by being balanced in the amount of time you are spending with them.

W.
Wear the Clothes that She Buys You.

Wear the shirts, pants, underwear or socks that she gives you even if they *aren't exactly* what you would have picked out.

X.
Learn to Appreciate Her.

Make a list of ways in which you take your wife for granted. Ask her to help you develop the list if you really want to make a serious impression and prepare for change. Then, find different ways to avoid taking her for granted and make the change. Ask her for a generous time allotment to make the changes, but let her know that you will be trying very hard.

Y.
Always Clean Up Before Making Love to Her.
Shower, shave, brush your teeth and/or fix your hair before making love to her. This demonstrates value to her.

Z.
Pray for Appreciativeness
Pray that He will help you love your wife through acts of service and will purify your heart and make your motives pure. Pray that God will empower you and change your heart and spirit to one of being able to truly *appreciate* her in a loving and Godly way.

CHAPTER ONE

—∞—

Create and Continually Enhance Meaning and Value for Her

Loving and honoring our wives is a lifelong process that will be continuously challenging for us. We will be presented with a variety of situations and our challenge, at all times, is to "love and honor her as Christ loved the church."

One of the most important ways we can love and honor her is to consciously create and continually enhance meaning and value for her through our actions, behaviors and words. That means that we must take action and show her that we love her. We must reject the concept that "she already knows how I feel about her." NO! We must continuously show her, tell her and create situations where she can see and feel it!

Here are a few ideas and suggestions to begin that work:

1.
Pray for God's Help.

Ask God for ways that your spouse, unique as she is, could benefit from actions and behaviors on your part to create meaning and value for her. Be sensitive to His prodding on what you can do. Earnestly seek His leadership as you express your love to her. Her responses will give clues to you as to further behaviors and actions for you to consider.

2.
Be Faithful to Her.

This should not have to be written, but physically, emotionally, psychologically, relationally, sexually and every other way, be faithful to her! Never look lustfully at another woman—especially when you are with her. When you find yourself looking lustfully at another woman, confess your sin and ask God to forgive you and teach you to be faithful to her and Him. The goal of sexual purity is to discontinue this behavior completely, but especially don't do it when you are with her. Integrity is *from the inside out*!

3.
Immediately Acknowledge Her Position.

You don't have to understand, agree or even think about it. Learn to immediately acknowledge her position! Try to develop the skill of restating your understanding of her position and asking her to clarify your understanding. At first, this will be difficult, but you can learn to do this in a *non-defensive* way! You can acknowledge her position without understanding it, embracing it or agreeing with it.

4.
Never Humiliate Her.

If she told you she would meet you at the gym to workout with another couple and would bring your things...but forgot your tennis shoes, blow it off. Allow her the opportunity to be human. Don't humiliate her about it. Regardless of the details, there is *never* a good enough reason to humiliate her about *anything*!

5.
Have a Portrait Made.

Make an appointment at the local portrait studio for the two of you. Do it in the middle of the day so you can both get ready for it together. Then make a different time for the family. Frame the pictures and place them in prominent places.

6.
Cooperatively Make Holidays Special.

Extra special! Work together with all members of the family to create extra meaning and value for all holidays throughout the year. Appendix I contains a few suggestions for major holidays and how they could create extra meaning and value for the entire family—but especially your wife!

7.
Make Sure She Sits in the Front Seat.

Arrange for her to sit in the front seat of the car with you. Always arrange with the children that your wife will sit in the front seat when you drive. They can take turns sitting in the middle in front or they can take turns sitting by the window while she sits in the middle. But she will *always* sit in the front seat of the car!

8.
Learn to Respect Her Space...

...Especially in the kitchen. First, leave her alone when she is in the kitchen unless she clearly invites you to help with dinner, cookies, a cake, etc. Second, learn where *she* puts the utensils, bowls and other things so you can put them where *she* keeps them when you're unloading the dishwasher or helping to put up clean dishes. Finally, never do any major cleaning, rearranging or remodeling in the kitchen without her permission and or assistance! There are other *spaces* that may be important to her. Learn to respect her space!

9.
Always Make Her a Priority.

Work hard in every situation to show her that she is your highest priority. You must always consider her, her feelings, her opinion, her family, her job or whatever else. You must choose for her to be the single most important person in your life, whether she is actually with you in presence or not!

10.
Guard Her Integrity.

Never tell embarrassing *secrets* about her to your friends, co-workers, acquaintances or especially to strangers. Don't talk bad about her to others. Always protect and defend her integrity, even during difficult times.

11.
Accept Who She Is.

Learn to accept her as a gift from God. She isn't like you—she is unique to her own, unlike any other woman or person in the universe! Accept her just as she is and gently grow with her. Just as she is!

12.
Ask for Help in Honoring Her.
Make a Wife's Request Page (Appendix F). Ask your wife to choose things from this book that she would appreciate you doing or making a part of your expressions of love toward her. Record them on a sheet of paper and work on those first!

13.
Pray Together.
This may be the hardest step in your marriage. Even Godly couples experience difficulty making this a priority. But it is crucial. Dr. John Trent shares a startling statistic: The divorce rate for our society is 50% (1 out of every 2). When looking at people claiming to be Christians, the divorce rate is exactly the same—50%. However, when looking at couples claiming to be Christians who pray together every day (even so much as a *sentence prayer*), the divorce rate is much less than 1%. In fact, according to Dr. Trent, it is 1 divorce out of 1,052 marriages. Pray at meals, at bedtime, at church, etc. Pray with her about problems and situations that you are both facing individually, as a couple, with the children and as a family, etc.

14.
Show Gratitude for Her Family of Origin.
Her parents are the people responsible for bringing her into this world and allowing the opportunity for you to be with her. On your wife's birthday, send a card to them thanking them for having her. Be grateful to them and even suggest times you could be with them. Don't worry that you'll never measure up, try to accept them and honor them. Encourage your wife to call them. Encourage her to spend time with them. You should try to spend time with them, also.

15.
Show Gratitude for Your Own Family of Origin.
Deal with your own stuff. Work to heal and move beyond your *past.* Reconcile relationships with parents, siblings and others. Learn to

love, forgive and cherish your family. Work on this as much as possible with *someone else* to help you and hold you accountable to real change!

16.
Display Her Importance to Others.

Keep two pictures of her in your wallet—one that is more *posed* and one that is a fun snapshot. Take them out and show them often. Keep it *in front* of the pictures of your children.

17.
Support Her in Front of the Children.

Whether or not you agree with her position or decisions, support her. Then talk about the differences in private. If you think she has punished them too harshly or not harshly enough, still support her in front of the children. If you come to an agreement that is different than what was said to the children, go to them and say that you cooled off, talked about the situation and this is *our* decision. Don't be afraid to admit you made a mistake. Parenting takes two—you and her. Don't triangulate! And, most importantly, don't undermine each other or attack each other!

18.
Show Value for People That She Values.

Learn the names of her friends, their husbands' names, occupations, childrens' names, etc. and occasionally show an interest in how they are doing. Sometime, out of the clear blue, ask her about one of them. If you run into them at a movie, a restaurant or at the mall, call her friend by name and ask about her husband or kids. Work at making eye contact with your wife's friend and show a genuine interest in what they are talking about. Ask your wife about them by name sometime. Suggest to your wife that maybe you all could get together and play cards, go out to eat, go for a walk or do something together sometime. Offer to plan it, arrange for a sitter and call her friends. Don't do this with a motive that is manipulative. It must be done purely to create meaning and value for your wife. If you suggest it and she thinks it's a good idea but wants to plan it, allow her to do that!

19.
Value Her at Your Office!

Keep a picture of her prominently displayed on your desk, on the wall in your office or someplace at you work. A picture of her...*alone*! It's OK to have one of the two of you and one with the children, too, but it is important to have one of her by herself! Also take one of the notes or cards she has given to you previously and set it out on your desk. Don't hide your love for her. Don't overlook it or take it for granted. But use your discretion and remember, some things are meant to be kept private between the two of you. You should treasure and respect those things just as much, but *don't* share them with others. She may never see these things, but the way you value her when you are apart will be magnified when you are near her.

20.
Take Her Picture and Display It!

Regularly take her picture and hang it in a prominent place in your home. Occasionally, have a special picture made into a puzzle or a poster at a local photo shop. She'll say "Don't do it, stop!" But it means alot to her, so do it! Have fun with this one. Take fun pictures of her mowing the lawn, with her mouth full or on the phone. Take her picture often...then, display it!

21.
Be Accessible to Her—Always!

Always let her know how to reach you. Tell her where you will be and when you *might* be gone. Assure her that if your secretary tells her that you are busy, you will let her know to interrupt you for the call anyway. If you travel, get a pager. Find ways to be accessible to her in case of emergency or otherwise. Explain that you are doing this because you value her and that she is important to you *every moment of the day*, not just in bed. If you leave your office, even for a short time, let your secretary know where you're going and with whom just in case your wife calls. If you travel alot or meet with people alot, get in the practice of giving her a copy of your weekly schedule and talk to her about who the names are and why you are meeting with them.

22.
Never Bring Up Her Faults!

NEVER mention her faults or remind her of mistakes—especially in front of others. Don't even bring them up when you are fighting about an issue. *Learn to forgive, work to forget.* Learn to create and communicate the value to her. Learn to rebuild and empower her. Learn ways to build her self-esteem or self-confidence. We all have faults and we know them better than anyone. As you seek to forget hers, she'll have a model to forgive and forget yours. However, use your discretion. There is a place for kind, loving, gentle and open confrontation. Occasionally, there may be some things you want and need to talk to her about. Be gentle and learn to discern how and when to know the difference. Marriage is a container for sanctification and "open rebuke is better than hidden love," but it must be done lovingly and sensitively. Never hold something against her or punish her for something she said or did. Let it go! Think about the relative importance of piddly things. Don't jeopardize the atmosphere of the relationship for something that wasn't *important.*

23.
Remember Dates!

Always remember dates which are important to her. Simple ones like her birthday, your anniversary, kids' birthdays, parents' birthdays, etc. are easier to remember. But you should even remember difficult ones like birthdays or anniversaries of the death of loved ones. Send her a note of encouragement and go out of your way to comfort her on those days, too. Get a calendar and ask her to help you to mark important dates throughout the year. Be responsible and transfer them from one year to the next (Appendix D).

24.
NEVER Bring Up Past Sins.

Seek help from pastoral staff, accountability groups or professional counseling to learn to heal past mistakes and forgive. But don't ever continuously throw up past mistakes. Let them go! They'll ruin a relationship fast! Learn to forgive and let them go. Practice forgiving her. Do a word search through the Bible on forgiveness and then apply it to your marital relationship—past, present or future! Be very quick to forgive and let past disappointments go, and don't bring them up! It doesn't matter how bad or how small they are.

They are all the same size in God's eyes and we are to forgive as He has forgiven us!

25.
Remember Your Anniversary.
It's important to her and it should be to you. Make it special! This is the person you are spending your entire life with! Buy her a card and a gift. Make a big deal out of this "holiday."

26.
Remember Her Birthday.
Before she reminds you it is coming up, remind her that a special day is coming. Make it fun for her! Create a *season of celebration* and give her a card each day of the week leading up to her birthday. Try to find extra ways to make her birthday special, and don't do the same thing each year. Be creative and create a celebration that she'll never forget!

27.
Don't Ever Compare Her!
Especially to another woman in a negative way. This includes your mother, previous girlfriends, friends or co-workers. You should try to never compare her to another woman even in a positive way. It's not smart! It's damaging! Don't EVER do it!

28.
Repeat Your Wedding Vows Often.
As often as you can, tell her if you had to do it all over again you'd choose her again. Be ready, she may not be quite as sure. Continually promise and reassure her that your love for her and faithfulness to her is "'til death do us part." Always come back to the basics: Commitment, communication, conflict resolution and physical touch. Repeat your wedding vows and recommit to the relationship regularly! Write out new vows and have them framed.

29.
Make Difficult Birthdays Special.
Especially 25th, 30th, 40th and 50th birthdays. Every morning during the week prior to her birthday, give her a gift. It doesn't have to be big and expensive, just make it something special. Then, on the

morning of her birthday, give her a poem that you have written for her. In advance, send a request to a list of her friends to remember to call on that special day.

30.
Ask Her to Help You.
Ask her to tell you how she wants and desires to be loved. Seek to love her in that way. Ask her what "quality time" means to her and then seek to create the value for her in that way.

31.
Value the Differences Between You.
Learn to acknowledge, accept and respect the differences in the way that you and your wife think, feel, speak, eat, sleep and care for children and etc. How boring and stale it would be if two people were exactly alike (or even close).

32.
Commit to Something of Importance to Her.
Make a time and/or a financial commitment to do something that means alot to her. Go on a mission trip with the church, volunteer at the school or work for a community organization.

33.
Spend Weekly Family Time!
Make one night a week "family night" to do something as a family. Take turns deciding who will choose what to do that night for this week, what to eat for dinner, etc. Make a chart and post three months at a time on the refrigerator. Even let the younger children feel that their input is valuable....

34.
Eat Together.
Don't start eating a meal until she sits down. Don't leave the table until she has finished eating. Don't eat in front of the television!

35.
Talk About Decisions with Her BEFORE a Decision is Made.

Always discuss minor issues and major decisions with her *prior* to making a commitment. Think about alternatives and let her give her input. Be attentive, respectful of her perspective, etc.

36.
Flirt with Her.

Flirt with her in public, at a party or social function. Try to make people think you are acting as if you are in love! Go up to her at a store after she has wandered off and approach her flirting and ask if she is married. Try "Excuse me, ma'am, I've been watching you a few minutes and I must say that you are the most beautiful woman in this store....Can I buy you a coke and get to know you?" Try to make the clerk blush! Then, if she says yes, buy her a coke and get to know her better. Let her know you love her *even when others are around*.

37.
Value the Notes She Gives You.

Keep the notes that she writes you in a file or box or something. Occasionally get them out and read them, telling her again how much they mean to you now more than ever.

38.
Dream Together.

Every couple of months, ask her to spend an hour or two with you just *dreaming*. Ask her where she wants to travel, if money was not an issue, or what kind of house she would like, etc. Just spend time dreaming, *together*. Some of the ideas, however, can become long term goals! Write out the dreams and continually update and change them. Learn the art of dreaming and involve her in every aspect of it. Set some goals and occasionally accomplish a "dream."

39.
Value Valuables!

Go to the local bank and lease a safety deposit box. Put birth certificates, important papers, insurance information, special family photos and keepsakes for the children in it.

40.
Attend a Marital Workshop Together.
Encourage her to attend a marital workshop with you. Take the initiative to find one. Make arrangements. Find childcare. Do it even if your marriage is great! Find ways to receive input and make it better! Purchase a Christian video series and watch it together. Share it with friends. Do this together with another couple, if you both can agree to do so. (See Appendix J for a list of resources and Appendix H for organizations which hold marriage workshops.)

41.
Accept and Treasure Her Love.
Learn to accept the love that she offers in the way that she offers it—no exceptions, modifications or demands! Learn to grow together.

42.
Help Her Make a List of Her Wants and Needs.
Constantly keep it before you. Focus on providing her requests.

43.
Put Your Arm Around Her in Public.
Act like you like her.

44.
Ask Her to Give You Input About You.
Seek her input on areas that pertain to changes in your life. For example, ask her, "Honey, what are three things you would change about me if you could change anything you want?" *Don't be defensive* and listen to what she says.

45.
Set Family Goals.
Set some goals and keep a list updated and posted to be seen everyday by everyone. Break down categories to what members of the family must do in order to have a realistic goal accomplished.

46.
Develop Couple-Friends.
Plan at least one night a month to spend with another couple going out and developing a relationship. Play cards, games, dance or just dinner

and talk. Try exchanging kids for a weekend. You keep their kids t. weekend and then you can go for a couple of days next month.

47.
Share with Her What You are Reading.

Tell her what it is about. Why are you reading it? What key points are you getting out of the book? How can she expect to see it make a difference in you? Talk to her as an intelligent human being. Ask for her input.

48.
Begin a Parenting Care Group.

Once a month, invite other parents over to your house for discussion, exchanging fresh ideas or to help other parents and couples with parenting issues. The purpose is to develop some support network to help *care* for one another and help each other. Plan some activities together. Utilize each other for babysitting on an evening or a weekend.

49.
Create a Legacy for Your Children.

Share your values in a tangible way. Try pictures in photo albums, yearly portraits down the hallway, journal entries once a month or something. Think of a unique way and make it a priority to record their lives so you can share it with them and their children.

50.
Make a List of Your Wants and Needs.

Give it to her and forget that it ever existed (unless she brings it up). Don't keep score, either.

51.
Talk About Your Childhood.

Tell your wife and children about your childhood memories. Teach them values *and* value creation. Help them understand the concept of "heritage" and help them understand theirs (which includes the two of you!). Take them and show them where you and your wife lived when you were growing up, attending school, going to church, etc. Take them to worship in your home church. This is very important!

CHAPTER TWO
—∾—

Encourage Her with Your Words

Have you ever worked really hard on a project at work and, finally, your boss acknowledges your work and gives you some verbal, public recognition? Do you remember that feeling of appreciation, affirmation and encouragement?

That is precisely what we must do as a husband for our wife. We should appreciate, affirm and encourage our wife in such a way that she feels that sense of worth and value becoming of her.

This section on encouraging words is simply intended to communicate value to your wife in a way she loves and needs—through oral and written communication.

52.
Ask God to Help You.
Ask God to help you know how to encourage her in ways that are meaningful to her.

53.
Begin and End Each Day Assuring Her of Your Love.
Start every morning, for seven-day stretches, with a different phrase, such as, "Good morning, honey, I love you!" or, "I love you more this morning than yesterday!" Do the same at bedtime. A day hemmed in expressions of love is less likely to unravel.

54.
Send Her Fun Messages of Love.
See the "Candy Bar Ideas" in Appendix C. Make up your own fun ways. Try to reinstill the joy you once shared with her into your relationship again.

55.
Write a List of Reasons Why You Love Her.
Think about it for weeks and try to make at least 25 items that are relevant (See Appendix A). "How do I love thee? Let me count the ways..."

56.
Say "Please" Alot.
Don't make assumptions. Don't always take things for granted. Learn to use your words and *ask* by saying "please": "Please pass the ketchup." "Honey, would you please iron my shirt before the meeting in two days." "Sweetheart, could we sit down and talk about money, please?"

57.
Say "Thank You" More Often.
Think you say it enough? Do it more. Learn how to and regularly practice expressing your appreciation with your words. Every day, find something that she has done and thank her for it!

58.
Be Gentle, But Honest with Her.
Especially about the clothes she is wearing when she asks you what you think. Tell her if her slip is showing, if she has a string hanging from the back of her blouse, something between her teeth, if a hair is out of place, etc. Be gentle and loving about it, but be honest. When something is bothering her and she asks to talk about it, don't be co-dependent and "take care of her." Rather, speak the truth in love. Not "speak the truth...love her." Speak the truth *in* love.

59.
Say "I Love You" an Awful Lot!
You can never say it too much, if you say it with sincerity. Tell her "I love you" until she is sick of hearing it or blue in the face, whichever

comes first. Say it when you *feel* overwhelmed by your emotions for her. Say it when you *don't feel* like saying it. Say it when she expects it. Say it when she doesn't expect it. Say it when she calls you on the phone. Say it before she leaves for work. Say it after a fight, before a fight, during a fight—Just say it!

60.
Tell Her How Young and Beautiful She Looks and Is...

...*Before* she asks, "Honey, how do I look?" But if she does ask before you can say anything, work extra hard to say convincingly, "Honey, you look gorgeous! I love it when your wear that blue dress," (be sure she has on a blue dress). Or, "You look so nice in that pant-suit!" Be honest, don't lie! And be very specific about how her dress highlights her hair (or whatever). Find something to compliment her on! But don't just affirm her beauty on the outside, seek to affirm her *beauty* on the inside, too. However, if you pour this on too thick, she'll stop believing you. So work to find the middle ground.

61.
Compliment Her Cooking.

Make very specific comments: "Honey, these are the best mashed potatoes I have *ever* eaten!" "This roast is so tender. Wow, you are a marvelous cook!" Compare it to being much "better than mom's." Learn to compliment her and tell her such things! However, sincerity is crucial and a necessity. Sometimes, just tell her "Honey, thanks for preparing a *good* meal" and *don't* say how wonderful it was, unless it was! Say what you mean and mean what you say. Just learn to say something positive. Deep down, she knows what the meal tasted like. And if you go on and on about how wonderful it was and she knows it wasn't, she may tend to doubt your sincerity on other things. This is a tough *art* and you must work at it!

62.
Be Positive in Talking to Her.

Learn to make positive comments and offer your feedback in a positive way. Usually the things that frustrate us about our spouse are those things that we initially fell in love with them over. For example, if you feel frustrated by the way she talks on the phone to her friends all the time, tell her, "Honey, I admire the way you conduct your friendships. You are very committed to them. And even though it is difficult at times for me, I appreciate the example you set for me to have in my friendships." Try to change your paradigm or perspective by choice. It will take time to make it habit.

63.
Ask Her to Clarify What She is Saying.
Don't always assume that you know what she is trying to say. Ask her to clarify it until you can understand. Use a phrase like, "Do I hear you saying...?" "What I hear is this....Is that accurate?"

64.
Regularly Give Her a List of Reasons Why "I Love You."
Don't photocopy the same list each time. Don't be repetitive, either. Make it a point to tell her different reasons why you love her. Write them in ink in your own handwriting and make them very personal and special. This is very time-intensive work and will take your undivided attention. Be very specific and personal. Invest in the relationship that you'll be in for the rest of your life. Not everyone is a writer and that's OK. But, written expression is very important to a woman. So try to leave a brief note and say a few words. Then, work at developing this art. It is important! Before long, you'll be more comfortable writing her and she'll *especially* appreciate how difficult it must be for you.

65.
Be Thankful and Grateful for Good Times.
Write her a note the morning after you went out, made love or spent time together as a family and let her know how much you appreciate her, love her and are proud of her. Something like, "Honey, last night was wonderful! Thank you for the evening!" Or, "Sweetheart, I am so proud of the way you parent our children. Thank you for sharing that part of you with us! I love you!"

66.
Constantly Write Notes.
Regularly write her a note or a letter telling her how much you love her, appreciate her, are proud of her, support her or something. Write her notes so that SHE KNOWS IT! Be honest, direct and

very specific. Again, even if writing comes difficult for you, don't blow this suggestion off! It will mean even more to her if you do something that appears difficult for you to do. Try to work on it. We keep mentioning the different ways to do this because it is very important and means alot to a woman!

67.
Sing an Answering Machine Message to Her.

If you have an answering machine, call home when you know she is gone and sing a song message to her. Make it something meaningful, such as: "I just called to say I love you." "Have I told you lately that I love you." "I love you more today than yesterday." Or even, "You are my sunshine!"

68.
Adore Her with Your Words.

Occasionally bow on your knees before her and praise her. Try to start for 30 seconds and work up to three solid minutes. Use phrases like, "You are..." and, "You deserve..." (See Appendix E). Too much? Try it, you'll know if it means anything to her. If you work hard at reading about loving her and honoring your marriage, it makes sense. (Thanks, Gary Smalley!)

69.
Write Her Notes for Each Day When She Goes on a Trip.

If she will be gone over the weekend, write her a note for each evening—Friday and Saturday. Place each respective note in a separate envelope with instructions on when to open it. Write her a note of encouragement for her presentation, her visit or her interview. Tell her you are proud of her and support her regardless. Tell her you cannot wait for her to be back home.

70.
Leave Paper Trails of Your Love!

Get in the practice of leaving her simple and brief notes of your love. On her pillow, under the covers, on the bathroom mirror, on her car steering wheel, on the kitchen table, on the front screen-door handle, etc. This will be even more meaningful to her if you have difficulty expressing your love to her in writing because she will know how vulnerable you may feel or how hard it must be for you. Try to learn to write her notes.

71.
Create a Barrage of Encouragement.
Send her friends a letter several weeks prior to her birthday asking them to make a special year for her, without saying you asked them to. Ask them to write, call, send letters or express appreciation to her, etc. Don't tell her you did it (unless she asks).

72.
Send a Card to Her at the Office
or Place of Work...Even If That is in the Home.
Make it special because *she will show it* to her friends or co-workers.

73.
Make Her a Unique Card.
Go to a local Hallmark card shop, Wal-Mart or other store (Target, Party Shop, etc.) and make her a personalized greeting card using a machine. Write her name on it and make it very special. Or, if you are artistic, make your own from scratch! None of these ideas are dependent on money. It's the thought and effort that she will appreciate anyway. Make it on the back of a napkin and put it under her silverware at dinner. Be creative!

74.
Call Her By a Nickname.
Find a nickname that she likes and call her that. Call her "Angel," "Darling," "Honey," "Sweetheart," or something else that is meaningful to her and instills value from you. Don't even play with a name like "chubby," "stick," etc! Avoid names like "Old lady." Although some are culturally acceptable, find something that builds her self-image and is a positive one. And remember, men, what you call her when she is not around still reflects your heart and reflects the honor that is (or is not) present for her!

75.
Tell Her You are Proud of Her.
Regularly write her a note telling her how proud you are of her. Leave it on the bathroom mirror or on the dining room table, under

her windshield wiper, etc. Sometimes, even leave it where your children will see it and read how much you love her and are proud of her.

76.
Tell Her How Wonderful She Is.

Tell your friends, especially mutual friends, how wonderful she is—in front of her. Be genuine and *real* for you! In other words, you may be the kind of husband that would impress your friends just by introducing her! You don't have to incredibly flatter her to tell others how wonderful you think she is. Be consistent and practice this in private, too.

77.
Send a Note Home Through the Mail.

Receiving a letter is very special to a woman! Send it with a stamp through the postal service. Or, if possible, send her a sweet message via e-mail. Sometimes include special thoughtful items such as a self-designed coupon good for a night of babysitting, a movie or whatever else is important to her. Send it to her even if she is a "homemaker."

78.
Remember the "Month" Anniversary.

Do this occasionally. For example, if you were married on January 20, 1994, buy her a card with a gift on March 20, 1996 on your 26th-month anniversary! Tell her how special she is and tell her you would do it all over again. Repeat your vows to her. But do this in addition to the yearly one. The yearly ones are very special and important!

79.
Write Her a Poem...

...Using words that you use every day. Make it genuine and expressive of who you are. Tape it on a mirror or dresser when you leave for work. Though you should do this frequently to make a believer of her, you can occasionally frame it. Come on, don't blow this off. It can be the most meaningful thing you do for her. Give it a try! It doesn't have to be perfect! And try to be a bit more creative than, "Roses are red, violets are blue, sugar is sweet and so are you."

CHAPTER THREE

Give Her Your Undivided Attention

Showing genuine interest and attentiveness to your wife is one of the most important ways to love and honor her. Undivided attention is imperative in any marriage—or relationship, for that matter—but it takes alot of practice to achieve.

Sometimes this will be very simple and come natural. Most often, though, it will be something that you must *train* yourself to do. Work hard at it and you will immediately see a difference that this will make in your marriage.

There is no easy way to do this. You must truly *choose* regularly to show her your undivided attention. And you must genuinely offer it!

80.
Allow God to Empower You to
Give Your Wife Undivided Attention.

Pray that God will help you to show her, one to one, her value to you. Don't allow yourself to be swayed to read the paper while talking to her. Or work on the car while asking her about her day. Ask God's help to make it a daily practice to focus directly on your wife and to practice this without fail!

81.
Make Eye Contact when You Talk!

You cannot show her value while you are talking to her while watching television, reading the paper, listening to a radio talk-show, etc. Make eye contact directly with her *every single time* you have a conversation with her. Remember, the eyes are the windows to the soul. Learn to make eye contact! *EVERY TIME!*

82.
Show Interest in Her Day!

Ask her how her day went. Then, sit and listen. Ask questions about little things and listen. Just *listen!* Encourage her. Show her that you are interested in what she is saying, doing, working on, etc.

83.
Spend One Night a Month Together with No Distractions.

Plan at least one regular night a month to spend together—just the two of you. Take her for a romantic dinner and movie. Try a love story, not a shoot-'em-up-and-kill-'em-type movie. Find something in your community to go to—an opera, community theater presentation, a play, a musical, etc. Again, if money is tight, don't worry about it, go window shopping or something. It is your undivided attention to her that honors her and communicates your love to her.

84.
Find Out Her Favorites.

Make a list of favorites that you want to know about her (See Appendix B). Type the list and give it to her to fill out. Then, try to memorize five new things each week about her. You'll be surprised how many times these will come up during normal conversation! Find out what she really likes at several of the favorite eating places around town. Then, surprise her at work or at home (wherever she works!) by taking her lunch. And take her something she really likes. Her friends will go nuts about how wonderful you are, and she'll be proud and appreciative! Learn about her. Find out as much as you can about this wonderful human being you are spending your life with.

85.
Buy Her Card in Advance of an Occasion.

In other words, buy her a card a week before her birthday, Valentine's Day or anniversary. To sweeten the anticipation, tell her a couple of times that you cannot wait for the special day to give her the special card. Provide numerous hints of your excitement. Make sure to have spent the time to find one that says something meaningful and relevant to her.

86.
Schedule Her Once a Week for Lunch...

...At least. Write it in your appointment book and allow nothing to make you late, forget or reschedule. Make it a priority and be on time! This can be a very special weekly time for the two of you!

87.
Send Her on a Scavenger Hunt.

Spend time arranging this first. Make child care and other necessary arrangements to clear an evening for the two of you. After you do the running around and setting this up, ask her to go to store #1 and pick up a package at the service counter.

1) *Store #1* could be a local bookstore. Have a package waiting for her at the front desk with a book that she would like—a novel, a calendar, a romantic book, etc.—with a note attached saying to stop by the florist at such-and-such address.

2) *Store #2* could be a florist where she will be handed a long stem rose with a note asking her to go to the lingerie store at the mall.

3) *Store #3* could be the lingerie store where they will give her your small, wrapped gift and a note telling her to meet you at such-and-such restaurant.

4) You will be waiting for her at the restaurant! Ask the hostess to greet her with a card from you and anticipate her arrival at an approximate time. Have the waiter or waitress ask for her drink order by calling her by her first name and provide excellent service for the special night.

Put some thought into this and make it something she will never forget!

88.
Always Hold Her Hand.

Ask her to go for a walk, then hold her hand. Hold it at the grocery store, on the walk between the car and the mall, at church, etc. When you are walking with the children, sometimes tell them that you cannot hold their hand right now because you want to hold your wife's.

89.
Reminisce Together!

Ask her to sit down and reminisce about the dating years. While doing it, ask her to sit on the couch beside you, like you did when you were first dating. Go back to some of the restaurants or places and relive some of that romance! Ask her to tell you about her high-school days and show some pictures, too.

90.
Ask Her For a Date.

Get in the habit of calling her and asking her to go somewhere for a party, etc., instead of *assuming.*

91.
Watch Her Dress and Undress.

Give her your undivided attention. Stare at her. Show her you adore her! Sometimes this may lead to more playful things, but don't always *expect* it. Remember, expectations can truly ruin a marriage.

92.
Read a Book Together.

Read ten pages a night or one chapter a week and then discuss it. If reading is difficult for you, let her read out loud. Or buy a "book on tape." Especially find a book on marriage, communication, parenting, fathering, etc. See Appendix H for information on additional resources, or find a book from the list in Appendix J.

93.
Shop Garage Sales Together.

Hey, you can save alot of money at yard sales and garage sales! It helps in being a good steward with *all* that God gives us! Besides that, it is really alot of fun! You can save alot of money and get some great deals, too!

94.
Snuggle and Read Song of Solomon.
Sit on the couch and snuggle a while. Then, get out your Bible and read together. Song of Solomon is a very intimate, *romantic* and moving place to start.

95.
Walk in the Rain Together.
Go for a walk in the rain or just after it rains. Notice the feel, the smell, the freshness. Take off your shoes and play in the puddles.

96.
Plant a Garden Together.
Try roses, tomatoes or something appropriate for your situation.

97.
Watch the Stars at Night.
Get away from the lights of the city and look for stars, constellations, etc. Can you see the military satellites (going north to south) or weather satellites (going east to west)? Try it!

98.
Go for an Ice-cream Cone.
On a summer day, get an ice-cream cone and go for a walk at the park. Or just sit in the ice-cream store, make eye contact and talk.

99.
Fly a Kite.
Purchase, assemble and fly a kite together. Listen, kids or no kids, this is a fun thing to do together. Take a blanket so when the kite is flying high, you can lay together and watch it.

100.
Call for No Reason.
Call daily from work just to tell her that you were thinking about her.

101.
Talk About Her Job...
..As well as yours. Don't be intimidated if her job seems more interesting than yours. And don't make her feel bad if it's the other way

around. Just ask her about her job and show an interest in what she does! Yes, this includes women who work in the home. They, too, have a job and you can just as easily ask about it!

102.
Be Involved in Things Together!

Attend parent-teacher conferences, PTA meetings, community meetings, church functions and other involvements together *as a couple.*

103.
Work Puzzles Together.

Buy a jigsaw puzzle and work it together while listening to a CD, the radio or audio tape. Try doing the puzzles with nothing on in the background and just talk. Start with one that is more simple. Don't start with a 1,000-piece, flower garden puzzle.

104.
Spend Time in Nature!

Go camping together, either alone or with the children. Let her decide where to pitch the tent, what to eat, etc., and don't complain a single time. Go swimming if she wants. Tour a cave, go for walks, swing at the park or something—no complaints! However, sometimes she won't feel like making the decisions. In those cases, *you* be willing to make them, keeping in mind her likes and dislikes.

105.
Watch a Movie with Her.

Listen to her talk about a movie she would like to see. Then, go rent it and watch it with her. Make her some popcorn and a coke. If the phone rings, you get up and get it while she enjoys the movie and you serve her. Better yet, let the phone ring!

106.
Go Shopping for a Negligee Together.

Do this only if it is important to her. Don't push your own agenda for sex onto her in this way or she will resent it.

107.
Spend a Work Day with Her.

Use annual leave, comp time or somehow take off from work one entire day to spend completely with her. If you have a good relationship with her boss, contact that person and *make arrangements* with him/her for your wife to take off. Treat her to a great day and never remind her of the sacrifice you have made.

108.
Put Your Arm Around Her at the Movie.
She'll love it and you'll be more comfortable, too.

109.
Exercise Together Regularly.
Ride bikes, join a health club, go swimming, walking or jogging.

110.
Go on a Picnic Together...
...Complete with sandwiches (that *you* made), chips, drinks, blankets, tape player, bikes, etc.

111.
Play at the Park.
Go to a local park and play together. Swing, run, throw a frisbee, have a picnic, sit and talk on a park bench, etc.

112.
Take Her to a Concert.
Buy tickets to a special concert and don't complain about the price. Find a group that was popular when you were dating or maybe a group that you both liked when you were younger. Choose her favorite group—a Christian concert or something—not yours!

113.
Take Her Dancing.
If this is something that doesn't have an inherent conflict with either of your belief systems, try it. Record six or eight songs on a tape and ask her to dance some quiet evening in the living room, den or bedroom. Invite other couples. Ask her to take dance lessons with you. If she likes country, offer to learn country. Not a single death has been reported listing "dance lessons" as a cause of death!

114.
Spend the Whole Day with Her.

Spend one entire day with her doing nothing except what she wants! Go shopping, drive through the countryside, work in the yard, etc.

115.
Paint Her Fingernails and Toenails.

CHAPTER FOUR

Serve Her and Share Responsibilities

Serving your wife might appear to be something very different than sharing household or family responsibilities. However, many men either fail to do one, the other or both.

Our argument is that we must serve her as though she matters. We must make her matter more than anything! *At the same time*, we must share the responsibilities as we seek to love and honor our wife. Though different concepts, they are, perhaps, inseparable.

The irony is that it is also a responsibility that we have in caring for ourselves and carrying our own weight with responsibilities.

As a side note, Dr. James Dobson suggests that the best way to enhance your *love life* with your wife might well be to help with household chores and responsibilities.

We challenge you to try it—serve and share.

116.
Ask the Ultimate Servant Model for Help.

"When you ask, you do not receive, because you ask with the wrong motive..." says James 4:3. Don't ask God to help you serve her and share the responsibilities so that your sex life will increase. Ask Him to help you to serve her and love her because it pleases Him. He can show you ways to love and honor her through serving.

117.
Make a Menu Together.

Sit down together and make a menu and corresponding grocery list together. Then delegate shopping responsibilities or shop together, but don't assume it is always her job to buy the groceries and prepare the meals!

118.
Create and Administer a Monthly Budget.

Discuss the monthly finances each month. Allow each other to give appropriate input, consider alternatives, make decisions and write checks. Remember to add in your church support, money for her to purchase her things and enough discretionary income to have freedom and flexibility in financial decisions. But, be smart and seek professional help if necessary in setting up a budget.

119.
Bring Home Dinner.

Call her at her place of work—even if that is in the home—and suggest bringing home dinner. Call her early enough that she doesn't already have something thawing or cooking. Stop on your way home and pick something up. When you get home, remove it from the boxes, set the table and serve it as though you worked all day preparing it.

120.
Discuss the Children Often.

Regularly sit and discuss the children's happiness, school, friends, behavior, future, clothes, rooms, toys, etc. What do you think needs improvement? How can you get there from where they are now? Regularly talk to your wife about the "cute" things that the kids are saying and doing. Discuss their fears. Talk about parameters that may need to be changed or environments that may need to be modified. Tap into your wife's natural ability to discern the children's social, emotional and psychological sensitivities. It will enhance your intimacy in the marriage, it will be meaningful to your wife, it will help your children, and it will allow you to grow in your fathering.

121.
Let Her Lay Down for a Nap.

Then, stay close to the phone to answer it and tell the caller she will call them back in a couple of hours. Stay near to the children to help them and care for them so that they don't disturb her rest, either. Answer the door, keep the television or radio volume on low, etc. *Do this on a regular basis.*

122.
Clean Off Her Car on Cold Days.
Scrape the ice and snow off of her car and warm it up for her without her having to ask. Try to do it without her even knowing you did it.

123.
Pretend You are a Waiter.
Fix the meal she wants, set the table, fix her drink, wait on her if she needs refills, sauce, salt and pepper or whatever. Put a towel in your waistband to role-play the part.

124.
Let Her Sleep in Late on a Regular Basis.
You assume the responsibility to allow her to rest as long as she wants/needs. No hassles and don't be a martyr!

125.
Perform "Honey-do's" at Your Own Home.
Take a full day and do nothing but fix items around the house. And never complain about it. Even allow her to change her mind and ask you to undo something you have just completed. Let her tell you how she wants something done. Make this a priority like you would if a neighbor called. You do it for everyone else in town, why not do it for your wife?

126.
Wait on Her!
Get her a refill on the drink, serve her a portion onto her plate, fix her drink, dessert, etc. At home, at the restaurant or at a guest's home. If someone says, "Pass the ketchup," you get it.

127.
Play Games with the Children Together.
Play games that are age-appropriate and chosen by the children, not your preference. Candyland, Don't Go To Jail, Jenga or Chutes and Ladders for the young ones. Monopoly, Clue, Don't Go to Jail or Jenga

for the older ones. Try different games. Ask friends what they use and be open to try *change*. Better yet, make up your own games! Be creative and explore available resources at a craft store.

128.
Secure the House at Bedtime.
Assure that *all doors and windows are locked* before you go to bed.

129.
Check on Things in the Middle of the Night.
Get out of bed in the middle of the night to see why the dog is barking, why the kids are crying or what the noise is.

130.
Care for Her Car.
Wash her car weekly and fill it up with gas, regardless of how dirty and how low the gas. Clean out the inside and wash the windows. Have the oil changed, add windshield-washer fluid, check the brake fluid, check the air pressure in her tires, etc.

131.
Wash Her Feet.
Gentlemen, this is the hardest of any act of love that you will ever try in your life, but it is the most meaningful if you share the faith. Jesus did it on very extra-special occasions and so can you. Buy a small tub at the discount store. Fill the tub with warm water, pick up a bar of soap, a washcloth and a towel. Read the Scripture as to what it means, why Jesus did it and how it was done by Jesus. Then, tell her, "Honey, this is awkward for me, but I want to try something very important." Dim the lights and do it. She'll probably cry as you serve her in the way of the Ultimate Servant and you will probably join her. *It is a very meaningful thing to do to honor and love her.* You'll get better as you do it, it'll get easier and she'll more than likely begin to do it back to you. It is very meaningful and eventually can involve the entire family. This is hard to start but is easy to do. It is probably one of the most meaningful things you can do to create biblical value in your spouse's life. *Try it.* Value her in this way!

132.
Take Out the Garbage...
...From the house to garage or from the garage to the curb regularly. Just do it without being asked. Replace the can liner, too.

133.
Sweep and Mop.
Sweep and mop the kitchen, bathroom or other bare floors, whether they are sticky or not.

134.
Clean Out and Scrub the Refrigerator.
Nobody, including her, wants to do this job...so why not you?

135.
Pick Up Your Dirty Clothes...
...And always put them in the designated hamper or basket. Carry the basket to the laundry room and do a load without being asked.

136.
Make the Bed Regularly.
It doesn't matter that you'll be getting in it later in the day. Make the bed. What is two minutes for her first thing in the morning?

137.
Clean the Oven.
First, ask her what kind of cleaner you should use. "Self-cleaning oven" doesn't mean it cleans itself. Also, change the tin foil under the burners on electric stoves. Did you even know that it was there? Guess how it gets changed. Go buy some new metal liners and start changing the tin foil yourself on a regular basis.

138.
Read the Kids a Story.
You volunteer to read the bedtime story to the children. This is your responsibility and it is a wonderful time to share their lives. This is important to kids and makes for a pleasant night's sleep. If they are scared about monsters and afraid to go to sleep, comfort them in a gentle, sensitive way. Leave them to go to sleep with the assurance of your unconditional love *every night*.

139.
Do the Laundry.
Tell her that you will be responsible for the laundry for an entire month. Then, be responsible for the entire month with *no complaints, reminders or faded shirts*! If you have a doubt as to whether something needs dry cleaning or other special care, *ask* first! If something needs ironing, learn to iron! Do it right without complaint!

140.
Wash the Dishes.
Make a commitment to wash the dishes every night that she cooks the meal. Then, keep your word for the entire week, month or whatever—with *no reminders*, etc. Load the dishwasher regularly!

141.
Clean the Bathroom on Your Own.
Don't wait to be asked, especially after shaving, cleaning the dog, washing filthy hands, etc. Just clean the sink, tub, floor, etc.

142.
Help to Bathe and Get the Kids Ready for Bed.
Be a responsible father.

143.
Share Meal Responsibilities.
Assume the responsibility of fixing dinner and cleaning up at least once a week. Make her a deal: When she cooks, you clean the kitchen and wash dishes. If you cook, she cleans the kitchen and does the dishes. Don't take meal time for granted. It is alot of work.

CHAPTER FIVE

Physically Adore, Honor and Love Her

"We would be alot happier if we had more sex or physical touch in this marriage!" We all have said it, and it is such a slam in the face of someone we love so much. It is very damaging and a cheap shot!

The art of physical touch is very meaningful and creates incredible positive energy in a marriage. But it is the art of physical touch and not just SEX. Physical touch, done in a loving and honoring way, creates a much deeper experience than the pure, sexual encounter.

Our wives are made, by the Creator, to be responders. So, in the event you are doing well with other parts of the book and you want ideas and suggestions to honor and love your wife through physical touch, read on.

144.
Pray for Guidance to Physically Love Her.
Two people know how to love your wife physically, to meet her needs, she and God. Ask Him to help you know how to love her through the physical touch and attention.

145.
ALWAYS Greet Her with a Kiss.

When you get home from work, the store, mowing the lawn or whatever, always greet her with a kiss and a hug for a few minutes immediately upon arriving home. Don't stop and adjust the mower, don't stop and shoot a basket, don't pull the weeds first or anything! Go straight to her, tell her hello and greet her, regardless of what your day was like, with a hug and a kiss!

146.
Touch Her Often.

When you walk by her, say something to her, talk about her, etc. Squeeze her knee gently, touch her cheek, touch her shoulder, run your fingers through her hair gently.

147.
Comfort Her.

Hold her when she cries and don't say anything—not one word! Just hold her, wipe her tears, hold her and wipe her tears, again.

148.
Help Her to Dress and Undress.

Zip her dress, help her with the necklace or bracelet, help her take off her boots, etc. Sometimes, offer to do it without waiting to be asked.

149.
Hold Her Tight when You Hold Her.

Every time you hold her!

150.
Learn to Hug...

...Not a "tee-pee" hug. Don't hug her with the type of hug that shoulders touch and that's it!

...Not an "old-lady" hug. Don't hug her like your great-grandmother hugs you.

...Not a "patting" hug. Don't hug her and softly pat her other shoulder.

Learn to hug intimately!

151.
Affirm Her in How She Wears Her Hair.
Don't tell her how to wear her hair. It's OK for you to suggest ways that you like it best, but don't put her down if she likes it different (or if she likes to regularly change it). However, always notice when she changes it, gets it cut or has it done! Let her know, in a positive way, that you notice!

152.
Scratch Her Back.
When she asks, scratch her back without complaining. But also offer to scratch it while you are watching a movie or sitting and talking on the couch or lying on the floor listening to the radio.

153.
Hug for 7 Seconds, Minimum.
Every single time you hug! Hug her for 7 seconds (at least) when you come home from work, while you kiss her, when you tell her goodnight in bed or whenever you hug! Do the 7-second hug every time you hug!

154.
Give Her a Massage.
Go to a local bookstore and purchase a book about massage. Read it. Then, ask her if you can give her a massage. Remember, it's for her gratification—not yours! Even if you just massage her feet or neck or arms or legs, do it on a regular basis. If you are short on time, massage only her shoulders or her face. Or, if she stands on her feet all day, massage her feet and legs. Try new things.
Generally speaking, it's not the benefit to the muscles, etc., it is the art of touching her in a loving and honoring way that we are suggesting here. There's not much of a way a man can mess that up, especially if listening to her requests. You may request for her to massage you more sternly. She may want the massage gentle and soft.

155.
Take a shower or a bath together.
Don't try to do the things that you want. Do what she wants—wash her back, wash her hair or whatever. Forget intercourse! Buy some

special soap or body lotion and surprise her with it. Run the water for her. Light a candle, fix her something to drink, put on soft music, etc., and love her in this way occasionally.

156.
Warm Up Her Side of the Bed.

Lie under the covers on her side of the bed to warm it up before she comes to bed. Then, when she comes into the room or gets beside the bed, roll over to the other side and let her experience the warmth.

157.
Learn How to Please Her while Making Love.

Ask her. Let her tell you what feels good and what brings her pleasure. Let her show you and teach you how to make love to her and with her.

158.
Accept that She Doesn't Have to Have an Orgasm to Enjoy Intercourse.

Women are different. She may have four or five an evening. She may not have any. For women, climaxes differ from one to the other and certainly differ from men. Learn her (not good English, but great advice)!

159.
Brush Her Hair.

Ask her to sit on the floor in front of you while watching a movie or listening to the tape or CD player, and brush her hair. Run the brush through it. Run your fingers through it. Learn the indentations of her scalp. Give her your undivided attention while doing this.

CHAPTER SIX

Shower Her with Gifts

Don't buy her gifts that you will share. Don't always buy her household gifts, either. Though not always bad, you should buy her personal gifts as well as practical ones. Both at the same time versus one or the other!

Select *meaningful* gifts, meaningful to her—and you! And remember, it is the time, thought and effort that you spend finding and selecting her gifts that will mean alot to her.

160.
Seek Wisdom from Above
in Showering Her with Gifts.

Gifts are important. But ask for God to help you select meaningful gifts that will meet needs and desires that your wife has. Pray for guidance. Pray for God to show you ways to express your love through meaningful gifts and to receive her love through receiving her gifts.

161.
Remember, It's the Thought
that Counts, NOT the Amount!

Keep in mind, gifts don't have to be large or expensive to be meaningful and honor her. It doesn't matter how much money you have or don't have! The cost of the gift is not important to your wife.

162.
Be Creative!

Use your imagination and find a unique way to honor and love her that isn't found in this booklet and regularly practice it! Our lives are all so unique and there are many ways you can listen to your wife and find individualized ways of honoring and loving her. (Then, write us and tell so we can pass it on!)

163.
Send Her Flowers for a Reason.

Flowers are great when she does something extra special at home, for her birthday, on your anniversary, when she has a bad day, or when you shared an especially nice weekend. Find a great reason to send her flowers.

164.
Treat Her to a Massage.

Buy her a certificate for a therapeutic massage at least once a month. Many fine hair salons have therapists, or look in the yellow pages.

165.
Show Her Value Through Fun Ways!

Buy her a candy bar and write her a note incorporating the name of the candy bar into some special message. For example, buy her a "$100,000 dollar bar." Write her a note telling her that she makes you feel like a hundred grand and give it to her during church, at lunch or at work! Before you leave on an overnight trip, give her a sack with a bunch inside (see Appendix C). Only *you* can think of the most meaningful surprises your wife would like.

166.
Send Her Away For a Retreat.

Help her to arrange a retreat to get away by herself for a couple of days. Maybe go and see a college girlfriend, or shopping trip. Just a get-away.

167.
Hire Some Outside Cleaning Assistance.

Hire a maid service to come in once a month and do a thorough house cleaning. Pay them to do some of the difficult and time-consuming work like cleaning windows, scrubbing baseboards and other hard things that take alot of time. Talk about this first and ask permission to do it for her.

168.
Dedicate Something to Her.
A book, a ball game, a story or letter.

169.
Buy a Gift Certificate for a Pedicure/Manicure.
This may not make sense to you—just do it. Many fine hair salons have specialists available for this reason, or look in the yellow pages. Get her a gift certificate and include a note with it to tell her she deserves to be pampered!

170.
Give Meaningful Gifts to Her.
Select meaningful things to give her as gifts. Find out something of interest and purchase those things for her. For example: angelic figurines, earrings, a book, bracelets or a bird house.

171.
Make a Tape of Her Favorite Songs, Not Yours!
Or you can make her a tape of love songs, expressive of your love for her and to her—some slow, some fast, some Disney tunes, pop tunes, rythym and blues, top-forty, etc. Be creative! Go to a local record store, borrow albums, tapes, CD's or whatever from friends. Spend time making it very personal and special.

172.
Help Her to Collect Something.
Ask her what she wants to collect and go out of your way to find times that you can purchase things for her. Support her buying things for herself, too.

173.
Send Her Flowers for No Reason.
"Just to say I love you!" or, "Just because." Send them to her work

(even if that is in the home) sometimes. Or stop and pick them up on your way home. Go for doughnuts on Saturday morning and come home with doughnuts and flowers!

174.
Regularly Fix Her Breakfast in Bed.

At bare minimum, take her a glass of juice or cup of coffee. Even if she says no, do it anyway. Carry it in to her when she wakes up. Don't forget the silverware and napkins.

175.
Regularly Do Little Extras.

On your way home from work, buy her a special favorite or treat at the bakery and surprise her with it. Get in the habit of doing extras.

176.
Buy Her a Dress for No Reason.

Women are unique. Buy her items that she likes such as a birdhouse, spoons or something that she collects. Buy her something that would make her happy. Buy her what she likes. Think about what your wife would like and buy it for her. But, occasionally, go out and find a beautiful dress that she would like, write a note with it, wrap it and give it to her.

CHAPTER SEVEN

Just Because You Love Her

Some things really don't matter. But because she's your wife and you love her, do them. *Just because you love her.*
Do you need ask more?

177.
Pray.
"God, help me to know how to love my wife and, in every little thing that happens in my relationship, help me to sort through what matters from what doesn't. Help me to love my wife as 'Christ loved the church' and do it for the same reason—just because. I know this pleases you, Father God!"

178.
Don't Drop Surprises in Front of Others.
Never let her hear that something significant *has* happened to you or is *about* to happen to you from a secretary, in a Bible study, at church, on the phone with someone else or with friends. Always tell her directly the very first thing! Choose to spend your life with her first.

179.
Ask and Listen.
Ask her how her day went and then sit and listen *attentively*. Turn off the television, turn off the radio, put down the newspaper—ask,

then listen attentively! Over a period of time, you'll learn more about her and will really grow to enjoy and appreciate this time.

180.
Call Her Before You Leave Work.
Call her from work before you leave to see if you need to stop at the store for milk, bread or anything.

181.
Allow Her to Comfort You.
Ask her to hold you when you cry, when you feel bad or when you have had a bad day and allow her to wipe *your* tears.

182.
Read About What Her Make up is Like.
Buy a few books about the sociological, psychological, emotional and physiological differences between men and women. Then, display an understanding of them (See Appendix J).

183.
Don't Make Her Feel Bad About Money!
Don't remind her of the disparity of proportion of income contributed to the household. Most men make more money than their wives. But what difference does it really make? Don't make her feel bad about buying special things for the house, gifts for the kids, her family, her friends, you or something for herself. Don't pour guilt on her for spending money on something that is important to her.

184.
Learn Ways to Fight Fair.
There are many books out about this. See a marriage counselor together, your pastoral staff or someone who can help you learn ways to discuss issues. Try to avoid words like "always," "never," etc. Instead, use "I feel as if...," or, "I'm angry because..."

185.
Agree to Disagree.
Accept the fact that sometimes the best you can hope for is to "agree to disagree." Learn to negotiate agreements on how to avoid certain topics. Every couple has these. Don't feel bad about it. Rather, learn

to accept that there are some topics or issues that are too sensitive to discuss without learning some advanced relationship and communication skills. *Seek to learn*!

186.
Squeeze the Toothpaste the Way She Likes It Squeezed.

187.
Never Try to Solve Her Situations.
Don't offer any advice as to how she could *fix* something at work or at church or with her friend. Support her and help her think of alternatives *only* if she asks you (then think twice still!).

188.
Walk at Her Pace.
When you go for a walk, slow down or speed up to meet her pace. Hey, if you're holding her hand or going to be opening the door for her, this is especially critical.

189.
Leave a Note When You Go On an Errand.
When she leaves the house to run an errand and you have to leave, always leave a note. "Honey, I ran to the store and will be right back. I love you! Me." Do so even if you talked to her about it and she knew you would be leaving.

190.
You Request a Counselor.
When you are struggling through difficult times in the relationship, *You* suggest seeing a minister/family counselor. Then, ask her who she might have in mind and negotiate someone without demanding. Deal with your pride later. Take the initiative—reach out and request a counselor or pastoral intervention (See Appendix H). Focus on the Family has a great referral service. Most of the others have toll-free numbers, too. Spend time exploring the resources out there!

191.
Help Her with Directions.
Help her to know the directions to her meeting by words that are

meaningful to her without making fun of her. We don't want to leave the wrong impression, but men and women are *different.* Just different. Men tend to use more words in directions, like: north, south, east, west, mile-marker numbers and more precise measurement because that's the way men tend to be. Women don't always use the same reference points as men. So recognize the difference. Try to communicate directions without making her feel like an idiot.

192.
Go with Her to Doctor Appointments.

Go with her for her annual checkup. Go with her for special concerns or x-rays. Ask her to go with you to yours or meet her at the doctor's office for the kids'. Especially if it is an important one, but even if it is a routine checkup, a physical or something simple...go with her.

193.
Go to Bed Together More Often than Not.

It is inevitable that your schedules will be somewhat conflicting. Some husbands like to go to bed late while some like to go to bed with young children, between 9:00 and 9:30 pm. Some wives like to stay up until midnight and get alot of work completed while kids are in bed. So learn to compromise and meet halfway. But go to bed *together* as much as possible. Try to lay in bed and talk to her while you are touching her or holding her, and don't have a sexual agenda all the time!

194.
Let Her Be the "T.V. Sheriff."

Ask her what television program she would like to watch and let her watch it! Give her the channel changer and allow her to flip channels at her own speed and stop wherever she wants to stop. Practice this often!

195.
Carry in the Groceries.

When she gets home from the store, unload the car for her. If a sack breaks, blow it off. Just pick up the items and the pieces and go on about unloading the car. Regularly offer to go shopping for/with her.

196.
Put Extra Covers on the Bed.
If she mentions how cold she is in bed on a regular basis, put an extra blanket on the bed without asking her. When you get into bed, just unfold your half and don't complain.

197.
Be a Gentleman on Brisk Nights.
Take off your coat and let her wear it on a brisk evening. Then, don't act cold. Suck up your gut and love her in this way. Put your arm around her, too.

198.
Call Her Every Single Night that You are Not Home.
Let her know what you are doing, who you are with, what your day was like, what your plans are, etc. Be sure to give her the message that you miss her and not the mistaken message of "checking-up" or "distrusting" her.

199.
Leave the Light on for Her.
When she is coming home after dark, make sure to leave the porch light, garage light and a light in the house on for her. Then, meet her at the door to welcome her home. Ask her how her day went and then sit and listen.

200.
Make a Sacrifice in Midseason.
Commit to her that, for one weekend, you will not sit and watch anything on television. For best results, make it in the dead-center of the football, basketball or baseball season. And don't remind her, complain or violate your word of your sacrifice.

201.
Leave for Work Early Without Disturbing Her.
Tell her that you will be especially quiet for one week while you get ready in the morning so that she can sleep. Then, be certain to set out everything that you need the night before so that you don't have to turn on the light or anything. Then remember to get everything

out of the room—shirt, pants, t-shirt, socks, shoes, tie, personal items—and move it all into another room the night before.

202.
Make a Will.

What would happen with your finances if you were to die? If she were to die? If one of the kids were to die? If you and she were both to die at the same time, who would take care of the children and how would they do it? Regularly, talk about it and update the will.

203.
Open the Door for Her.

Open the car door for her every single time you go somewhere with her. Hold the door open when you enter the restaurant. Every door you come to when your wife is with you—open it for her.

204.
Put the Toilet Seat Down when You're Finished.

Not the cover, the *seat*. Listen, between us men, it's *just as easy* for women to lift it as it is for men to put it down. But, because we love our wives, let's just agree to do this for them.

CHAPTER EIGHT

Additional Ideas

As you experience your own unique ways to love and honor your wife, write them down on the following few pages. Then, send your ideas to us and we will include them in reprints and revisions to help others. Remember, this is a working document that is intended to help men with "ideas and suggestions to love and honor their wives."

A-1.

_____ .

_____

_____

_____

_____

A-2.

_____ .

_____

_____

_____

_____

A-3.

_____ .

_____

_____

_____

_____

A-4.

_____ .

_____

_____

_____

A-5.

_____ .

_____

_____

_____

A-6.

_____ .

_____

_____

_____

How Do I Love Thee?

From idea #55.

I love you because.....Just because. I love you because of the way you treat me. I love you because you are the mother of my children...because of the way you love others...because of your love for Jesus...just because I love you. I love you because of your love for others...because you are beautiful...because of who you are on the inside...because you are a strong, loving woman...because you are gentle and loving...because you are so sweet. I love you because of your innocence...because you are so pure...because you are a gift from God...because I am a smart, grateful, man...because...I know a good thing when I see it!

Appendix B

List of Favorites

From idea #84.

Shoe size: _____
Date: _____
Sock size: _____
Pant size:_____
Panty/underwear size: _____
Bra size:_____
Shirt size: _____
Sweater size:_____
Dress size:_____
Eye color: _____
Coat size: _____
_____ : _____
_____ : _____
Favorite perfumes:
   1) _____
   2) _____
   3) _____
Favorite flower (type/color): _____
Favorite plant: _____
Favorite color: _____
Favorite candy bar: _____
Favorite candy:_____
Favorite food dishes: _____
   1) _____
   2) _____
   3) _____
Favorite seafood: _____
Favorite desserts: _____
   1) _____

2) _____
3) _____
Favorite restaurant in town: _____
_____

Favorite cereal: _____
Favorite cheese: _____
Favorite meat: _____
Favorite juice: _____
Favorite ice cream: _____
Favorite kind of doughnut: _____
Favorite kind of chips: _____
Favorite kind of pickle: _____
Favorite shape: _____
Favorite salad dressing: _____
Favorite cookies: _____
Favorite fruit: _____
Favorite vegetable: _____
Favorite Kool-Aid flavor: _____
Favorite grocery store: _____
Favorite general store: _____
Favorite holiday: _____
Favorite month: _____
Favorite day of the week: _____
Favorite year: _____
　　　　because: _____
_____

Favorite movie: _____
Favorite actress: _____
Favorite actor: _____
Favorite Bible person: _____
Favorite book in the Bible: _____
Favorite Bible verses:
　　　1) _____
　　　2) _____
　　　3) _____
Favorite boys' name: _____
Favorite girls' name: _____
Favorite relative: _____
Favorite kind of dog: _____

Very most favorite person in the world and why?

_____

Favorite music singer: _____

Favorite song:_____

Favorite vacation spot without kids: _____

Favorite vacation spot with kids: _____

Favorite camping spot: _____

Favorite friend: _____

Favorite person that she works with:_____

Favorite teacher that she's ever had: _____

Favorite grade in school:_____

People she considers to be "heroes":

      1) _____

      2) _____

      3) _____

Her favorite ways/desire to be loved:

      1) _____

      2) _____

      3) _____

Favorite names she likes to be called (other than given):

      1) _____

      2) _____

      3) _____

Her favorite gift ever received:

_____

Favorite birthday party ever:

_____

Favorite book ever started but not finished:

_____

Favorite book ever finished:

_____

Favorite Romantic Dinner:

_____

FAVORITE FOODS:

The following is a name-association/order game. First, read the name of the restaurant in the left-hand column. Then, write the "meal" that would be her preference from that restaurant in the right column:

Dairy Queen: _____

McDonald's: _____

Captain "D's": _____

Long John Silvers: _____

Hardees: _____

Taco Bell: _____

Sonic: _____

Pizza Hut: _____

The Olive Garden: _____

Kentucky Fried Chicken: _____

Denny's: _____

_____ : _____
_____ : _____
_____ : _____
_____ : _____
_____ : _____
_____ : _____
_____ : _____
_____ : _____
_____ : _____
_____ : _____
_____ : _____

Candy Bar Ideas

From ideas #54 and #165.

B uy a candy bar. Then, write a note and wrap it around the candy
bar and give it to her. Some samples:

1. Special Treasures
    "Honey, you are my 'special treasure.'"
2. Delights
    "You bring many 'delights' to my life!"
3. Symphony
    "Our love is a 'symphony' to me."
4. Good-'n-Plenty
    "I love you 'good-'n-plenty.'"
5. Sweet Tarts
    "You are my 'sweet tart!'"
6. Riesen
    "I have many 'riesens' to love you—here's one."
7. Everlasting Gobstoppers
    "My love for you is 'everlasting!'"
8. A can of nuts
    "I am 'nuts' for you!"
9. Almond Joy
    "You bring great 'joy' to my life."
10. $100,000 Bar
    "You're love is worth more than a 'hundred
    grand' to me!"
11. Life Savers
    "You are a 'life saver' to me."
12. Starburst
    "You are galaxies above all others and cause stars to burst
    in me."

13. Care-Free gum
    "Your love is 'care-free.'"
14. Nerds
    "I've been a 'nerd,' please forgive me."
15. Double mint gum
    "Your love is double-double, good-good.'"
16. beef jerky
    "Sweetie, I'm sorry I've been a 'jerk' lately."
17. Mounds
    "I have 'mounds' of love for you."
18. Twist & Shout
    "Being with you makes me 'twist & shout!'"

Use your own imagination—BE CREATIVE!

—∽∽—

Significant Dates

Sample from idea #23.

January
: 3—Amy's Birthday
13—Ben's Birthday
15—Daniel & Kim's Birthday
20—Laura & Bob's Wedding Anniversary
28—Bob's Birthday
30—Dana's Birthday

February
: 14—Valentine's Day

__—_____

__—_____

__—_____

March
: 9—Laura's Grandmother's Birthday
17—St. Patrick's Day
21—Grandma Vickers' Birthday

April
: 2—Don's Birthday
9—Laura and Bob's First-Date Anniversary
27—Andrew's Birthday

__—_____

__—_____

May
: 19—Audrey's Birthday
__—Mother's Day
22—Grandma's Birthday

__—_____

__—_____

June   __—Father's Day
                        10—Nick's Birthday

                        __—_____
                        __—_____

July   4—Vickers/Self/Weld Family Reunion
                        6—Mike's Birthday
                        12—Laura's Birthday
                        18—Janice's Birthday
                        21—Laura's Grandfather's Birthday

August   24—Dad's Birthday
                        30—Cindy's Birthday
                        30—Jeff's Birthday

                        __—_____
                        __—_____

September   12—Karen's Birthday (for kids)

                        __—_____
                        __—_____

October   1—Katie's Birthday
                        9—Bill's Birthday
                        11—Blossom's Birthday
                        25—Lindy's Birthday

November   3—Anniversary of Andrew's death (1988)
                        5—David's Birthday
                        8—Brenda's Birthday
                        13—Allison's Birthday
                        18—Mom's Birthday
                        15—PaPa's Birthday

December
                        21—Jeff/Dana's Anniversary
                        25—Christmas

Significant Dates

January

February

March

April

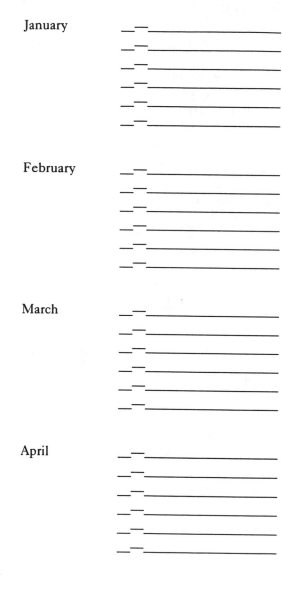

May

    __—_____

    __—_____

    __—_____

    __—_____

    __—_____

    __—_____

June

    __—_____

    __—_____

    __—_____

    __—_____

    __—_____

    __—_____

July

    __—_____

    __—_____

    __—_____

    __—_____

    __—_____

    __—_____

August

    __—_____

    __—_____

    __—_____

    __—_____

    __—_____

    __—_____

September   __—_____

               __—_____

               __—_____

               __—_____

               __—_____

               __—_____

October   __—_____

               __—_____

               __—_____

               __—_____

               __—_____

               __—_____

November   __—_____

               __—_____

               __—_____

               __—_____

               __—_____

               __—_____

December   __—_____

               __—_____

               __—_____

               __—_____

               __—_____

               __—_____

List of Affirmations

From idea #68

You are a worthy child of God...
You are a wonderful mother...
You are an honest woman...
You are a kind parent...
You are a very loving person...

You are worthy to minister anywhere...
You are a very strong person...
You are a spiritual being...
You are a precious soul...
You are a strong woman...

You are an intelligent woman...
You are a compassionate woman...
You are an admirable friend...
You are a good person...
You are a tremendous lover...
You know how to communicate in unique ways...
You are a sensitive friend...
You are a loyal person...
You are a persistent woman...
You are one of a kind...

There is no one in the world like you...
You are unique, standing head and shoulders above all other women...
You live your life as a testimony to the fact that you are a strong, loving woman...
You are a trusting and trustable person...

You are an attractive person...
You are a devoted mother, employee and friend...
You are human and worthy of making mistakes...
You are such a gentle lady...
You are very meek, yet strong...

You are worthy of respect and honor...
You are adorable in the eyes of man and God...
You are a totally complete woman worthy of respect...
You are a wise woman...
You are a very perceptive and sensitive lady...

You are a great teacher and a joyful learner...
You are a fun "player"...
You are not afraid to take risks...
You are a fragile woman worthy of tenderness...
You are a tender-hearted person...
You make mistakes and are imperfect, but are wise in acknowledging this...
You are such a thoughtful person...

You are a giving person...
You are considerate...
You are a great cook...
You are a creative person...

You are an attractive woman...
You are significant and matter to people...
You are needed...
You are greatly used in this world...
You are an accepting person...

You are a graceful woman...
You are capable and worthy of learning to pray and making significant contributions in the lives of people...
You are a successful freedom graduate...
You are a valuable asset to this world...

You are an expressive woman...
You are a sensual woman...

You know how to be accountable and practice it...
You know how to dream...
You know how to play and enjoy life...
You are a confident woman...

You are a humble servant of God...

Wife's Request Page

From idea #12

Priority Requests:

1. _____

2. _____

3. _____

4. _____

5. _____

Specific Requests:

I. Enhancing Meaning and Value: _____

II. Encouraging Words: _____

III. Undivided Attention: _____

IV. Serving and Sharing: _____

V. Physically: _____

VI. Gifts: _____

VII. Just Because: _____

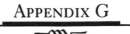

Universal Truths

From idea #B

Do's:

- Do commit your life to Christ! Seek to continually grow in your faith. Learn to pray and consistently pray. Get involved in a local New Testament Church. Seek to be obedient to Christ.

- Do commit to your wife for life, unconditionally!

- Do seek to understand before being understood.

- Do confess sin to your spouse.

- Do pray together about conflict!

- Do touch her alot.

- Do constantly tell her you love her.

- Do compliment her often.

- Do consistently build her self-esteem with positive affirmations.

- Do support her in public...whether she is with you or not.

- Do constantly practice patience in every aspect of your life (not just with her and your children).

- Do grow yourself. Consistently work on things you can change.

Don'ts:

- Don't attack character—only address behavior!
- Don't "mind read."
- Don't keep track of past offenses.
- Don't touch each other in anger!
- Don't say, "I can't change." Say, "I won't change," if you must say either!
- Don't say, "I'll try." Say, "I'll do it."
- Don't say you should or shouldn't. Say "I wish you would (or wouldn't)..."
- Don't remind her that you were right (even if you were!).
- Don't use the "D" word (Divorce).
- Don't say "you never" do this or that.
- Don't say "you always" do this or that.
- Don't go to bed with unresolved anger.
- Don't look at another woman lustfully...especially when you are with her.
- Don't ever compare her in a negative way.

Additional Resources

From ideas #B, #40, #92 and #190.

Gary Smalley @ Today's Family
1482 Lakeshore Drive
Branson, Missouri 65616   1-800-848-6329

Dennis and Barbara Rainey @ Family Life Marriage
Conferences (Affiliated with Campus Crusade for Christ)
PO Box 23840
Little Rock, Arkansas 72221-3840   1-800-FLTODAY

Dr. John Trent @ Encouraging Words
12629 North Tatum, Suite 208
Phoenix, Arizona 85032   1-800-900-8640

Dr. Ken Canfield @ The National Center for Fathering
10200 West 75th Street, Suite 267
Shawnee Mission, Kansas 66204   1-800-593-3237

Dr. James Dobson @ Focus on the Family
Colorado Springs, Colorado 80995   1-800-232-6459
   •Has counseling referral service and network.

Bishop TD Jakes @ The Potter's House
PO Box 5390
Dallas, Texas 75208   1-800-Bishop2

Dr. Jim Talley @ Relationship Resources, Inc.
11805 Sylvester Drive, Suite 100
Oklahoma City, Oklahoma 73162   (405) 789-2900

United Marriage Encounter   1-800-334-8920
National Campaign to Protect Marriage   (513) 733-8908
Marriage Watchers International   (303) 987-8583

—∽∽—

Making Holidays Special

From idea #6.

Thanksgiving

Prior to saying grace before the meal, ask each family member share something that they are thankful for that has happened during the past year. Either make or buy your wife a nice, thoughtful card expressing your "thankfulness" for all that she does throughout the year. Be creative to come up with a nice centerpiece for the table. You might get the traditional cornucopia or you might design one yourself using pictures and souvenirs of trips or fun things that you did during the past year that creates feelings of thankfulness. After the dinner, you clean the table, do the dishes and clean the kitchen.

Christmas

Whether you have children or not, create homemade ornaments. Give your wife a special ornament each year. Help her decorate the house, tree, yard, etc., in the way she would desire. Find a gift-line that you can begin building for your wife from one year to the next. Cooperatively select a couple of traditions that you both feel are important for your family to begin or continue.

New Years Eve

Invite a few couples over to celebrate the time together. Play games, cards or something for the evening. Involve the children if you have them. Lighten up. Pray the new year in, too.

Father's Day

Be appreciative for the things that she does for you on this special day. Write a "thank you" note for the gifts, dinner or whatever. Let her know how much you appreciate her making the day special for you.

Mother's Day

Pick a flower out of the garden for her to wear as a corsage. Make her breakfast in bed. Help the kids do something special for her.

Easter

Discuss what to buy the children for Easter. Buy her a dress or, at minimum, encourage her to get a new one if she wants. Be supportive of this special time for her. Learn about Passion Week and create family traditions to support the holiday season. Maybe read the story from the Bible. If Easter egg hunts are important for your young children, make the time special while coloring them. Take lots of pictures.

Book List

From ideas #B, #N, #40, #92 and #182.

Books on Tape:

Bradshaw, John. *Creating Love.* New York, NY: A Bantam Audio Cassette, 1992.

Gray, John. *What Your Mother Couldn't Tell You & Your Father Didn't Know.* New York, NY: Harper Audio, 1994.

———. *Men Are From Mars, Women Are From Venus.* New York, NY: Harper Audio, 1993.

———. *Mars and Venus in the Bedroom.* New York, NY: Harper Audio, 1993.

Smalley, Gary & John Trent, Ph.D. *The Hidden Value of a Man.* Irving, TX: BOOKTRAX Word Publishing, 1992.

———. *The Blessing.* Nashville, TN: Thomas Nelson Publishers, 1993.

Smalley, Gary. *Making Love Last Forever.* Dallas, TX: Word Publishing, 1996.

Books:

Backus, William & Marie Chapian. *Telling Yourself the Truth.* Minneapolis, MN: Bethany House Publishers, 1980.

Barr, Debbie. *Children of Divorce.* Grand Rapids, MI: Zondervan Publishing House, 1992.

Bolin, Dan & John Trent, Ph.D. *How to be Your Wife's Best Friend.* Colorado Springs, CO: Pinon Press, 1995.

Bugbee, Bruce; Don Cousins and Bill Hybels. *Network.* Grand Rapids, MI: Zondervan Publishing House, 1994.

Buscaglia, Leo E., Ph.D. *Loving Each Other.* New York, NY: Ballantine Books, 1984.

Canfield, Ken R. *The 7 Secrets of Effective Fathers.* Wheaton, IL: Tyndale House Publishers, Inc; 1992.

Canfield, Ken. *The Heart of a Father.* Chicago, IL: Northfield Publishing, 1996.

Chapman, Gary. *The Five Love Languages.* Chicago, IL: Northfield Publishing, 1992.

Covey, Stephen R. *The Seven Habits of Highly Effective People.* New York, NY: Simon & Schuster, 1989.

Exley, Richard. *The Making of a Man.* Tulsa, OK: Honor Books, 1993.

Gray, John. Men, *Women and Relationships.* Hillsboro, OR: Beyond Words Publishing, Inc; 1993.

Honor Books. *God's Little Instruction Book on Love.* Tulsa, OK: Honor Books, 1996.

Hughes, R. Kent. *Disciplines of a Godly Man.* Wheaton, IL: Crossway Books, 1991.

Jampolsky, Gerald G. *Love is Letting Go of Fear.* Berkeley, CA: Celestial Arts, 1979.

Janssen, Al and Larry K. Weeden, ed. *Seven Promises of a Promise Keeper.* Colorado Springs, CO: Focus on the Family Publishing, 1994.

Kreidman, Ellen. *Light Her Fire.* New York, NY: Dell Publishing, 1991.

Lewis, Gregg. *The Power of a Promise Kept: Life Stories.* Colorado Springs, CO: Focus on the Family Publishing, 1995.

Markman, Howard; Scott Stanley and Susan L. Blumberg. *Fighting for Your Marriage.* San Francisco, CA: Jossey-Bass Publishers.

McGee, Robert S. *The Search for Significance.* Houston, TX: Rapha Publishing, 1990.

McGinnis, Alan Loy. *The Friendship Factor.* Minneapolis, MN: Augsburg Publishing, 1979.

McCartney, Bill, ed. *What Makes a Man?* Colorado Springs, CO: NAVPRESS Publishing Group, 1992.

Rainey, Dennis and Barbara. *Building Your Mate's Self-Esteem.* San Bernardino, CA: Here's Life Publishing, Inc; 1986.

Sledge, Tim. *Making Peace with Your Past: Help for Adult Children of Dysfunctional Families.* Nashville, TN: LifeWay Press, 1992.

Smalley, Gary. *Joy That Lasts.* Grand Rapids, MI: Zondervan Publishing House, 1988.

————. *Hidden Keys of a Loving Lasting Marriage.* Grand Rapids, MI: Zondervan Publishing House, 1988.

Smalley, Gary & John Trent, Ph.D. *The Language of Love.* New York, NY: Pocket Books, 1988.

————. *The Blessing.* New York, NY: Pocket Books, 1986.

Swindoll, Charles R. *Strike the Original Match.* Portland, OR: Multnomath Press, 1980.

Talley, Jim, Ph.D. *Reconcilable Differences: Healing for Troubled Marriages.* Nashville, TN: Nelson Publishers, 1991.

Tannen, Deborah, Ph.D. *You Just Don't Understand.* New York, NY: Ballantine Books, 1990.

————. *That's Not What I Meant!* New York, NY: Ballantine Books, 1986.

Trent, John. *Love for All Seasons: Eight Ways to Nurture Intimacy.* Chicago, IL: Moody Press, 1996.

Viscott, David, M.D. *I Love You, Let's Work It Out.* New York, NY: Pocket Books, 1987.

Wagner, E. Glenn, Ph.D. *Strategies for a Successful Marriage.* Colorado Springs, CO: NAVPRESS Publishing, 1994.

Williamson, Marianne. *A Return to Love.* New York, NY: Harper Collins Publishers, 1992.

Wolgemuth, Robert. *She Calls Me Daddy.* Colorado Springs, CO: Focus on the Family Publishing, 1996.

Wright, H. Norman. *Quiet Times for Couples: A Daily Devotional.* Eugene, OR: Harvest House Publishers, 1990.

To order additional copies of

199 Ideas and Suggestions to Honor and Love Your Wife

Have your Visa, Mastercard, or Discover Card ready
and Call 1-800-917-BOOK
(operators on duty 24 hours a day)

For quantity discounts,
to send a "gift book" or set of "gift books" to a friend or relative,
to address the authors,
to request information on our grant-writing
service assisting not-for-profit organizations,
to inquire about our professional resume service,
or
for information on other books in the
Returning to the Basics in Relationships series including:

199 Ideas and Suggestions to
Honor and Love Your Wife,

199 Ideas and Suggestions to
Love and Respect Your Husband,

and others,

Call toll free 1-888-857-2993

or write to

Encouragement Builders
503 Nifong, Suite # 113
Columbia, Missouri 65205-6024

(The truths of our books are also available on audio cassette.)